D1065109

# I CAN'T FIGHT THIS FEELING

# I CAN'T FIGHT THIS FEELING

## Timeless Poems for Lovers
### from the Pop Hits of the '70s and '80s

Foreword by Fred Schneider of The B-52s

Edited by Danny Cassidy

**QUIRK BOOKS**
PHILADELPHIA

Library of Congress Cataloging in Publication Number:
2002091192

ISBN: 1-931686-11-4

Printed in Singapore

Typeset in Bauhaus and Blippo Black

Designed by Maria Taffera Lewis

Cover image © Tim Pannell/CORBIS

Additional copyright information begins on page 92

Distributed in North America by Chronicle Books
85 Second Street
San Francisco, CA 94105

10 9 8 7 6 5 4 3 2 1

Quirk Books
215 Church Street
Philadelphia, PA 19106
www.quirkbooks.com

# Contents

Foreword by Fred Schneider        7

I Honestly Love You – Olivia Newton-John        10

Brandy (You're a Fine Girl) – Looking Glass        12

Bad Medicine – Bon Jovi        15

I Think I Love You – The Partridge Family        18

Making Love Out of Nothing at All – Air Supply        20

Lady in Red – Chris de Burgh        23

Morning Train – Sheena Easton        25

Hot Stuff – Donna Summer        28

Guilty – Barbra Streisand and Barry Gibb        30

Hot Blooded – Foreigner        33

Can't Fight This Feeling – REO Speedwagon        36

Dance with Me – Orleans        38

More Than Words – Extreme        39

What About Love? – Heart        40

Hooked on a Feeling – B. J. Thomas        42

Take My Breath Away – Berlin        44

Sometimes When We Touch – Dan Hill        46

You're the Inspiration – Chicago        48

**Physical** – Olivia Newton-John    **50**

**Missing You** – John Waite    **52**

**Sweet Child O' Mine** – Guns N' Roses    **54**

**All Out of Love** – Air Supply    **56**

**Still the One** – Orleans    **59**

**Time After Time** – Cyndi Lauper    **62**

**Like a Virgin** – Madonna    **65**

**Woman in Love** – Barbra Streisand    **68**

**Sweet Emotion** – Aerosmith    **70**

**Glory of Love** – Peter Cetera    **71**

**Tonight I Celebrate My Love** –
Peabo Bryson and Roberta Flack    **72**

**We Belong** – Pat Benetar    **74**

**Have You Ever Really Loved a Woman?** –
Bryan Adams    **76**

**Islands in the Stream** –
Kenny Rogers and Dolly Parton    **78**

**Better Be Good to Me** – Tina Turner    **81**

**Afternoon Delight** – Starlight Vocal Band    **85**

**Can't Get Enough of Your Love, Babe** –
Barry White    **87**

**Index of First Lines**    **90**

**About the Authors**    **92**

# foreword

Y ou know a love song is destined for immortality when people start naming their pets—or even their children—after it. My friend Linda named her cat "Brandy" after the "fine girl" described in the popular Looking Glass song. Plenty of Neil Diamond fans have christened their daughters "Desiree," and I'm surprised there aren't more "Rhiannons" walking around nowadays.

Such is the power of a timeless love song. Though I'm not primarily known as a singer of love songs (unless you want to count "Quiche Lorraine"), I do enjoy a well-crafted ode to amour. And I can appreciate the work that goes into creating one: Many songwriters have tried to compose a tune that will last through the ages, but very, very few ever actually succeed.

Here, for your reading pleasure, is an anthology of the best—the most moving (or, at least, the most unusual) love poetry of the '70s and '80s. I realize some people might object to the format of this book; some might argue that the lyrics of Air Supply's "All Out of Love" don't merit the same treatment as John Milton's "Paradise Lost." But I disagree. I think the poetry of Air Supply—and other great pop stars—deserves to be immortalized in a hardcover anthology that lovers can cherish for generations. Here, at last, is just that book.

If you don't have a lover, the poems in **I Can't Fight This Feeling** can be a powerful aid in finding one. Ever since man (and woman) carved words into stone, people have employed verse in their romantic conquests—and the music of the '70s and '80s is the perfect tool for breaking down anyone's resistance. Today's liberated lady bent on seduction, for example, would do well to recite a few choice lines from Olivia Newton-John: "I wanna get physical / I wanna get animal / let me hear your body talk."

Men, on the other hand, will probably have more success with the discreet metaphor, like this subtle couplet from the Starlight Vocal Band: "You've got some bait a-waiting and I think I might / try nibbling a little afternoon delight."

These love poems will even help people whose relationships have lost their spark. Why not ignite your lover's skyrockets by letting Barry White do the talking—especially if you've already "shared love and made love and—there's just not enough of it" for you. Barry is the Maestro of Love—and reciting any of his lyrics will get you good results.

So open this book with your loved one and grab a seat next to the fireplace—just like those wonderfully romantic couples in the old K-tel commercials. Pour yourselves some wine. Take turns reading these poems to each other. Find that highway to the sky. Make it through the wilderness. Shine like a candle in the window on a cold, dark winter's night.

And me? I'll use the lyrics to "Physical" with a little "Hot Stuff" until, as Olivia Newton-John so poignantly describes on page 50, "there's nothing left to talk about, / unless it's horizontally."

—Fred Schneider

# I Honestly Love You

Olivia Newton-John

Maybe I hang around here
a little more than I should.
We both know I got somewhere else to go,
but I got something to tell you
that I never thought I would.
But I believe you really ought to know:

I love you.
I honestly love you.

You don't have to answer.
I see it in your eyes.
Maybe it was better left unsaid.

This is pure and simple,
and you must realize
that it's coming from my heart
and not my head:
I love you.
I honestly love you.

I'm not trying to make you feel uncomfortable.
I'm not trying to make you anything at all.

But this feeling doesn't come along every day,
and you shouldn't blow the chance
when you've got the chance to say:

I love you. I love you.
I honestly love you.

If we both were born
in another place and time,
this moment might be ending in a kiss.

But there you are with yours,
and here I am with mine,
so I guess we'll just be leaving it at this:

I love you.
I honestly love you.

# Brandy (You're a Fine Girl)

## Looking Glass

There's a port
on a Western bay,
and it serves
a hundred ships a day.

Lonely sailors
pass the time away
and talk about their homes.

There's a girl
in this harbor town,
and she works
laying whiskey down.
They say, "Brandy,
fetch another round."
She serves them whiskey and wine.

They say, they say,
"Brandy,
you're a fine girl.
What a good wife
you would be.
Yeah, your eyes could steal a sailor from the sea."

Brandy

    wears a braided chain
made of finer silver
    from the north of Spain.
A locket
    that bears the name
of a man that Brandy loves.

He came
    on a summer's day
bringing gifts
    from far away.
But he made it clear
    he couldn't stay.
No harbor was his home.

He said, he said,
    "Brandy,
you're a fine girl.
    What a good wife
you would be.
    But my life, my lover, my lady, is the sea."

Yeah, Brandy used to watch his eyes
    when he told his sailing stories.
She could feel the ocean fall and rise.
    She saw its rage and glory.

But he had always told the truth.

Lord, he was an honest man,

and Brandy does her best to understand.

At night,

when the bars close down,

Brandy walks through

the silent town,

and loves a man who's not around.

She still can hear him say, she hears him say,

"Brandy,

you're a fine girl.

What a good wife

you would be.

But my life, my lover, my lady, is the sea."

# Bad Medicine

Bon Jovi


Your love is like bad medicine.

    Bad medicine is what I need.

Shake it up, just like bad medicine.

    There ain't no doctor that can cure my disease.


I ain't got a fever, got a permanent disease.

    It'll take more than a doctor to prescribe a remedy.

I got lots of money but it isn't what I need.

    Gonna take more than a shot to get this poison out of me.

    Yeah, I got all the symptoms—count 'em: one, two, three.

    First, I need.
    That's what you get for falling in love.

    Then, you bleed.
    You get a little but it's never enough.

    And then you're on your knees.
    That's what you get for falling in love.
    And now this boy's addicted cause your kiss is the drug.


Your love is like bad medicine.

Bad medicine is what I need.

Shake it up, just like bad medicine.

There ain't no doctor that can cure my disease.

Bad, bad medicine.


I don't need no needle to be giving me a thrill.

And I don't need no anesthesia or a nurse to bring a pill.

I got a dirty down addiction. It doesn't leave a track.

I got a jones for your affection, like a monkey on my back.

There ain't no paramedic gonna save this heart attack.


When you need.

That's what you get for falling in love.

Then you bleed.

You get a little but it's never enough.


And then you're on your knees.

That's what you get for falling in love.

Now I'm addicted and your kiss is the drug.


Your love is like bad medicine.

Bad medicine is what I need.

Shake it up, just like bad medicine.

So let's play doctor, baby,

cure my disease.

Bad, bad medicine

   is what I want.

Bad, bad medicine

   is what I need.


I need a respirator 'cause I'm running out of breath.

   You're an all night generator wrapped in stockings and a dress.

When you find your medicine you take what you can get,

   cause if there's something better baby,

well, they haven't found it yet.

# I Think I Love You

## The Partridge Family

I'm sleeping,
   and right in the middle of a good dream,
      I call out once I wake up,
      from something that keeps knocking at my brain.
   Before I go insane, I hold my pillow to my head
      and spring up in my bed,
         screaming out the words I dread:
         "I think I love you."

This morning,
   I woke up with this feeling
      I didn't know how to deal with.
      And so I just decided to myself
   I'd hide it to myself and never talk about it,
      and did not go and shout it
         when you walked into the room:
         "I think I love you."

I think I love you,
   so what am I so afraid of?
      I'm afraid that I'm not sure of
      a love there is no cure for.
   I think I love you.

Isn't that what life is made of?
    Though it worries me to say
that I'd never felt this way.


I don't know what I'm up against.
    I don't know what it's all about.
I've got so much to think about.


Hey, I think I love you,
    so what am I so afraid of?
        I'm afraid that I'm not sure of
    a love there is no cure for.
I think I love you.
    Isn't that what life is made of?
        So it worries me to say
    I never felt this way.


Believe me, you really don't have to worry;
    I only want to make you happy.
        And if you say, "Hey, go away," I will.
    But I think better still,
I better stay around and love you.
    Do you think I have a case?
        Let me ask you to your face:
    "Do you think you love me?"


Oh, I think I love you.

# Making Love Out of Nothing at All

## Air Supply

I know just how to whisper
　　and I know just how to cry.
I know just where to find the answers
　　and I know just how to lie.

I know just how to fake it
　　and I know just how to scheme.
I know just when to face the truth
　　and then I know just when to dream.

And I know just where to touch you
　　and I know just what to prove.
I know when to pull you closer
　　and I know when to let you loose.

And I know the night is fading
　　and I know the time's gonna fly.
And I'm never gonna tell you everything I gotta tell you
　　but I know I gotta give it a try.

And I know the roads to riches,
　　and I know the ways to fame.

I know all the rules and then I know how to break them
and I always know the name of the game.

But I don't know how to leave you
and I'll never let you fall.
And I don't know how you do it,
making love out of nothing at all.

Making love out of nothing at all.
Making love out of nothing at all.
Making love out of nothing at all.

Every time I see you all the rays of the sun
are streaming through the waves in your hair.
And every star in the sky
is taking aim at your eyes like a spotlight.

The beating of my heart is a drum
and it's lost, and it's looking for a rhythm like you.
You can take the darkness from the pit of the night
and turn it to a beacon burning endlessly bright.

I've gotta follow it, 'cause everything I know, well
it's nothing till I give it to you.

I can make the runner stumble.

  I can make the final block.

And I can make every tackle at the sound of the whistle.

  I can make all the stadiums rock.


I can make tonight forever,

  or I can make it disappear by the dawn.

And I can make you every promise that has ever been made

  and I can make all your demons be gone.


But I'm never gonna make it without you.

  Do you really wanna see me crawl?

And I'm never gonna make it like you do,

  making love out of nothing at all.

Making love out of nothing at all.

Making love out of nothing at all.

Making love out of nothing at all.

# Lady in Red

Chris de Burgh

I've never seen you looking so lovely as you did tonight.

I've never seen you shine so bright.

I've never seen so many men ask you if you wanted to dance.

They're looking for a little romance,

given half a chance.

And I've never seen that dress you're wearing,

or the highlights in your hair that catch your eyes.

I have been blind.

The lady in red

is dancing with me,

cheek to cheek.

There's nobody here;

it's just you and me.

It's where I want to be.

But I hardly know

this beauty by my side;

I'll never forget

the way you look tonight.

I've never seen you looking so gorgeous as you did tonight.

I've never seen you shine so bright. You were amazing.

I've never seen so many people want to be there by your side.

And when you turned to me

and smiled, you took my breath away.

I have never had such a feeling

(such a feeling of complete and utter love),

as I do tonight.


The lady in red

is dancing with me,

cheek to cheek.

There's nobody here;

it's just you and me.

It's where I want to be.


But I hardly know

this beauty by my side;

I never will forget the way you look tonight.

The lady in red, my lady in red.


I love you.

# Morning Train

Sheena Easton

i wake
up every morning.
i stumble

out of
bed
stretching
and a-yawning
another day

ahead. it seems
to last
forever
and time
will slowly ride

'til babe and me's
together—
then it starts
to fly. because the
moment
that he's with me,

time can take
a flight. the
moment
that he's with me,
everything's
all right. night-

time is the right time. we make
love. then it's his and my
time—we take up. my baby

takes the morning
train. he works from nine
to five, and then he
takes another
home again, to find

me waiting for him. he
takes me to a movie, or
to a restaurant. to go slow-
dancing. anything

i want. only when he's with me,
i catch a light. only what
he gives me makes me feel
all right. all day,

i think of him, dreaming
of him, constantly.
i'm crazy, mad
for him, and he's
crazy, mad for me.
when he steps off

the train, i meet him before
the fight. work all day
to earn his pay,
so we can play

all night.

# Hot Stuff

Donna Summer


Sitting here, eating my heart out, waiting—
    waiting for some love to call.
Dialed about a thousand numbers lately,
    almost rang the phone off the wall.


Looking for some hot stuff, baby, this evening.
    I need some hot stuff, baby, tonight.
    I want some hot stuff, baby, this evening.
Gotta have some hot stuff.
    Gotta have some love tonight.


I need some hot stuff. I want some hot stuff.


I need hot stuff.


Looking for a lover who needs another.
    Don't want another night on my own.
Wanna share my love with a warm-blooded lover;
    wanna bring a wild man back home.

Gotta have some hot love, baby, this evening.

I need some hot stuff, baby, tonight.

I want some hot stuff, baby, this evening.

Gotta have some lovin'—got to have love tonight.


I need hot stuff.

Hot love—looking for hot love.


How's about some hot stuff, baby, this evening?

I need some hot stuff, baby, tonight.

Looking for my hot stuff, baby, this evening.

I need some hot stuff, baby, tonight.

Yeah, yeah, I want some hot stuff, baby, this evening.

I want some hot stuff, baby, tonight—

# Guilty

Barbra Streisand and Barry Gibb

Shadows falling, baby,
we stand alone.
Out on the street
anybody you meet
got a heartache of their own.

(It ought to be illegal.)
Make it a crime to be lonely
or sad.
(It ought to be illegal.)

You got a reason for living.
You battle on.
With the love you're living on,
you gotta be mine.
We take it away.
It's gotta be night and day.
Just a matter of time.

And we got nothing to be guilty of. Our love
will climb any mountain.
Near or far, we are.
And we never let it end.

We are devotion.
And we got nothing to be
sorry for. Our love
is one in a million.
Eyes can see that we got a highway to the sky.

Pulses racing, darling:
How grand we are.
Little by little,
we meet in the middle.
There's danger in the dark.

(It ought to be illegal.)
Make it a crime to be out
in the cold.
(It ought to be illegal.)

You got a reason for living.
You battle on.
With the love you're building on,
you gotta be mine.
We take it away.
It's gotta be night and day,
just a matter of time.
And we got nothing to be guilty of. Our love
will climb any mountain.
Near or far, we are.

And we never let it end.

We are devotion.

And we got nothing to be

sorry for. Our love

is one in a million.

Eyes can see that we got a highway to the sky.

I don't want to hear your

goodbye.


Don't want to hear your

goodbye.

# Hot Blooded

foreigner

Well, I'm hot blooded.

Check it and see.

I got a fever of a hundred and three.

Come on baby,

do you do more than dance?

I'm hot blooded,

I'm hot blooded.

You don't have to read my mind,

to know what I have in mind.

Honey, you oughta know.

Now you move so fine,

let me lay it on the line.

I wanna know what you're doin' after the show.

Now it's up to you,

we can make a secret rendezvous.

Just me and you,

I'll show you lovin' like you never knew.

That's why I'm hot blooded.

Check it and see.
I got a fever of a hundred and three.

Come on baby,
Do you do more than dance?
I'm hot blooded,
I'm hot blooded.

If it feels all right,
   maybe you can stay all night?
Shall I leave you my key?

But you've got to give me a sign.
   Come on, girl,
some kind of sign.
   Tell me, are you hot, mama?
   You sure look that way to me.

Are you old enough?
   Will you be ready when I call your bluff?
Is my timing right?
   Did you save your love for me tonight?

Yeah, I'm hot blooded,
check it and see.
Feel the fever burning inside of me.

Come on, baby,

do you do more than dance?

I'm hot blooded,

I'm hot blooded.


Now it's up to you:

Can we make a secret rendezvous?

Before we do,

you'll have to get away from you-know-who.


Hot blooded,

every night.

Hot blooded,

you're looking so tight.

Hot blooded,

now you're driving me wild.

Hot blooded,

I'm so hot-blooded hot for you, child.

Hot blooded,

I'm a little bit high.

Hot blooded,

you're a little bit shy.

Hot blooded,

you're making me sing.

Hot blooded,

for your hot blooded sweet sweet thing.

# Can't Fight This Feeling

## REO Speedwagon

I can't fight this feeling any longer,
   and yet I'm still afraid to let it flow.
What started out as friendship has grown stronger—
   I only wish I had the strength to let it show.

I tell myself that I can't hold out forever.
   I say there is no reason for my fear,
because I feel so secure when we're together.
   You give my life direction.
   You make everything so clear.

And even as I wander,
   I'm keeping you in sight.
You're a candle in the window
   on a cold, dark winter's night.
And I'm getting closer than I ever thought I might.

And I can't fight this feeling anymore.
   I've forgotten what I've started fighting for.
It's time to bring this ship into the shore
   and throw away the oars forever.
Cause I can't fight this feeling anymore.

I've forgotten what I've started fighting for.
And if I have to crawl upon the floor
   or come crashing through the door—
   Baby, I can't fight this feeling anymore.

My life has been such a whirlwind since I saw you.
   I've been running 'round in circles in my mind.
And it always seems that I'm following you, girl,
   cause you take me to the places
   that alone I'd never find.

And even as I wander,
   I'm keeping you in sight.
You're a candle in the window
   on a cold, dark winter's night.
And I'm getting closer than I ever thought I might.

And I can't fight this feeling anymore.
   I've forgotten what I've started fighting for.
It's time to bring this ship into the shore
   and throw away the oars forever.

Cause I can't fight this feeling anymore.
   I've forgotten what I've started fighting for.
And if I have to crawl upon the floor
   or come crashing through the door—
   Baby, I can't fight this feeling anymore.

# Dance with Me

Orleans

Dance with me, I want to be your partner.

Can't you see the music is just starting?

Night is falling, and I am calling. Dance with me.

Fantasy could never be so giving. I feel free.

I hope that you are willing. Pick your feet up,

and kick your feet up. Dance with me.

Let it lift you off the ground

Starry eyes, and love is all around.

I can take you where you want to go.

Dance with me, I want to be your partner.

Can't you see the music is just starting?

Night is falling, and I am calling.

Dance with me.

# More Than Words

Extreme

Saying "I love you" is not the words I want to hear from you.
It's not that I want you not to say, but if you only knew
how easy it would be to show me how you feel,
more than words is all you have to do to make it real.
Then you wouldn't have to say that you love me,
'cause I'd already know. What would you do if my
heart was torn in two? More than words to show you feel
that your love for me is real. What would you say if I took those
words away? Then you couldn't make things new just by saying
"I love you."
La di da da di da. More than words.
Now that I have tried to talk
to you and make you understand,
all you have to do is close your eyes
and just reach out your hands and touch me,
hold me close. Don't ever let me go.
More than words is all I ever needed you to show.
Then you wouldn't have to say that you love me,
'cause I'd already know—

# What About Love?

Heart

I've been lonely.

    I've been waiting for you.

I'm pretending

    and that's all I can do.


The love I'm sending

    Ain't making it through to your heart.


You've been hiding—

    never letting it show.

Always trying

    to keep it under control.

You got it down

    and you're well on the way to the top.

But there's something that you forgot:


What about love?

Don't you want someone to care about you?

What about love?

Don't let it slip away.

What about love?

I only want to share it with you.

You might need it some day—

I can't tell you
    what you're feeling inside.
I can't sell you
    what you don't want to buy.
Something's missing
    and you got to look back on your life.
You know something here just ain't right.


What about love?
Don't you want someone to care about you?
What about love?
Don't let it slip away.
What about love?
I only want to share it with you.

# Hooked on a feeling

B. J. Thomas

I can't stop this feeling deep inside of me.
    Girl, you just don't realize what you do to me.
When you hold me in your arms so tight,
    you let me know everything's all right.

I'm hooked on a feeling.
I'm high on believing
that you're in love with me.

Lips as sweet as candy—
    its taste is on my mind.
Girl, you got me thirsty
    for another cup of wine.
I got a bug from you, girl,
    but I don't need no cure;
I'll just stay a victim
    if I can't restore.

All the good love
    when we're all alone—
keep it up, girl,
    yeah, you turn me on.

I'm hooked on a feeling.
I'm high on believing
that you're in love with me.

I'm hooked on a feeling,
and I'm high on believing
that you're in love with me.

I said I'm hooked on a feeling,
and I'm high on believing
that you're in love with me.

# Take My Breath Away

Berlin

Watching every motion in my foolish lover's game.
On this endless ocean, finally, lovers know no shame.

Turning and returning
to some secret place inside.
Watching in slow motion
as you turn around and say,
   "Take my breath away.
   Take my breath away."

Watching, I keep waiting,
still anticipating
love. Never hesitating
to become the fated ones.

Turning and returning
to some secret place inside.
Watching in slow motion
as you turn to me and say,
   "Take my breath away.
   Take my breath away."

Through the hourglass I saw you.
In time, you slipped away.
When the mirror crashed, I called you.
And turned to hear you say,

"If only for today, I am unafraid.
Take my breath away. Take my breath away."

Watching every motion
in this foolish lover's game.
Haunted by the notion,
somewhere there's a love in flames.

Turning and returning
to some secret place inside.
Watching in slow motion
as you turn my way and say,

"My love, take my breath away.
My love, take my breath away."

# Sometimes When We Touch

Dan Hill

You ask me if I love you,
   and I choke on my reply.
I'd rather hurt you honestly
   than mislead you with a lie.
And who am I to judge you
   on what you say or do?
I'm only just beginning
   to see the real you.

And sometimes when we touch,
   the honesty's too much,
And I have to close my eyes and hide.
   I want to hold you 'til I die,
'til we both break down and cry,
   I want to hold you
   'til the fear in me subsides.

Romance and all its strategy
   leaves me battling with my pride.
But through the insecurity
   some tenderness survives.
I'm just another writer,

still trapped within my truths;
a hesitant prize fighter,
   still trapped within my youth.


At times I'd like to break you,
   and drive you to your knees.
At times I'd like to break through,
   and hold you endlessly.
At times I understand you,
   and I see how hard you've tried.
I've watched while love commands you,
   and I've watched love pass you by.
At times I think we're drifters,
   still searching for a friend,
a brother or a sister,
   but then the passion flares again.


And sometimes when we touch,
   the honesty's too much,
And I have to close my eyes and hide.
   I want to hold you 'til I die,
'til we both break down and cry,
   I want to hold you
      'til the fear in me subsides.

# You're the Inspiration

Chicago

You know our love was meant to be
   the kind of love that lasts forever.
      And I want you here with me
      from tonight until the end of time.
You should know, everywhere I go
   you're always on my mind, in my heart, in my soul, baby.

You're the meaning in my life.
   You're the inspiration.
You bring feeling to my life.
   You're the inspiration.
I want to have you near me,
   I want to have you hear me saying,
"No one needs you more than I need you."
   (No one needs you more than I.)

And I know (yes I know) that it's plain to see;
   we're so in love when we're together.
      Now I know (now I know) that I need you here with me
   from tonight until the end of time.
You should know, everywhere I go,
   you're always on my mind, in my heart, in my soul, baby.

You're the meaning in my life.

    You're the inspiration.

You bring feeling to my life.

    You're the inspiration.

I want to have you near me,

    I want to have you hear me saying,

"No one needs you more than I need you."

    (No one needs you more than I.)


When you love somebody until the end of time—

When you love somebody, always on my mind—

No one needs you more than I—

# Physical

## Olivia Newton-John

I'm saying all the things that I know you'll like.
  Making good conversation,
  I've got to handle you just right.
  You know what I mean.
I took you to an intimate restaurant,
  then to a suggestive movie.
  There's nothing left to talk about,
  unless it's horizontally.

Let's get physical, physical.
  I wanna get physical.
    Let's get into physical.
  Let me hear your body talk, your body talk.
    Let me hear your body talk.

I've been patient, I've been good.
  [I] tried to keep my hands on the table.
  It's getting hard—this holding back
  (if you know what I mean).
I'm sure you'll understand my point of view.
  We know each other mentally.
  You gotta know that you're bringing out
  the animal in me.

Let's get physical, physical.

    I wanna get physical.

        Let's get into physical.

    Let me hear your body talk, your body talk.

      Let me hear your body talk.


Let's get animal, animal.

    I wanna get animal.

        Let's get into animal.

    Let me hear your body talk.

      Let me hear your body talk.

# Missing You

John Waite

Every time I think of you,
    I always catch my breath.
And I'm still standing here and you're miles away,
    and I'm wondering why you left.
And there's a storm that's raging
    through my frozen heart tonight.

I hear your name in certain circles
    and it always makes me smile.
I spend my time thinking about you,
    and it's almost driving me wild.
And there's a heart that's breaking
    down this long distance line tonight.

I ain't missing you at all
    since you've been gone away.
I ain't missing you
    no matter what I might say.

There's a message in the wild,
    and I'm sending you this signal tonight.
You don't know how desperate I've become,

and it looks like I'm losing this fight.
In your world, I have no meaning,
   though I'm trying hard to understand.
And it's my heart that's breaking
   down this long distance line tonight.

I ain't missing you at all
   since you've been gone away.
I ain't missing you no matter
   what my friends say.

And there's a message that I'm sending out
   like a telegraph to your soul.
And if I can't bridge this distance,
   stop this heartbreak overload!

I ain't missing you at all
   since you've been gone away.
I ain't missing you no matter
   what my friends say.

I ain't missing you.
I ain't missing you—

# Sweet Child O' Mine

## Guns N' Roses

She's got a smile that it seems to me
reminds me of childhood memories
where everything was as fresh as the bright blue sky.

Now and then, when I see her face,
she takes me away to that special place,
and if I stared too long, I'd probably break down and cry.

Ohhhhh, oh oh,
sweet child o' mine.
Ohhhh, oh, oh, oh,
sweet love of mine.

She's got eyes of the bluest skies,
as if they thought of rain.
I hate to look into those eyes
and see an ounce of pain.

Her hair reminds me of a warm safe place
where as a child I'd hide,
and pray for the thunder and the rain
to quietly pass me by.

Ohhhhh, oh oh,
sweet child o' mine.
Ohhhh, oh, oh, oh,
sweet love of mine.

Where do we go?
Where do we go now?
Where do we go,
Sweet child o' mine?

# All Out of Love

## Air Supply

I'm lying alone
with my head on the phone,
thinking of you 'til it hurts.

I know you hurt too,
but what else can we do?
Tormented and torn apart.

I wish I could carry
your smile in my heart,
for times when my life feels so low.

It would make me believe
what tomorrow could bring,
when today doesn't really know—
doesn't really know.

I'm all out of love.
I'm so lost without you.
I know you were right
believing for so long.
I'm all out of love.

What am I without you?
I can't be too late
to say that I was so wrong.

I want you to come back
and carry me home,
away from these long lonely nights.

I'm reaching for you.
Are you feeling it, too?
Does the feeling seem oh so right?

And what would you say
if I called on you now
and said that I can't hold on?

There's no easy way.
It gets harder each day.
Please love me or I'll be gone—
I'll be gone.

I'm all out of love.
I'm so lost without you.
I know you were right
believing for so long.
I'm all out of love.

What am I without you?
I can't be too late
to say that I was so wrong.

Oh, what are you thinking of?
What are you thinking of?
Oh, what are you thinking of?
What are you thinking of?

I'm all out of love.
I'm so lost without you.
I know you were right
believing for so long.
I'm all out of love.
What am I without you?
I can't be too late—
I know I was so wrong.

# Still the One

Orleans

We've been together since way back when.
Sometimes I
never want to see you again.
But I want you to know,
after all these years,
you're still the one
I want whisperin' in my ear.

You're still the one
I want to talk to in bed.
Still the one
that turns my head.
We're still having fun,
and you're still the one.

I looked at your face every day
but I never
saw it 'til I went away.
When winter came,
I just wanted to go
deep in the desert.
I longed for the snow.

You're still the one
that makes me laugh
Still the one
that's my better half.
We're still having fun,
and you're still the one.

You're still the one
that makes me strong
Still the one
I want to take along.
We're still having fun,
and you're still the one.
Yes, you are.

Changing, our love is going gold.
Even though we grow old, it grows new.

You're still the one
that I love to touch.
Still the one
and I can't get enough.
We're still having fun,
and you're still the one.

You're still the one
who can scratch my itch.
Still the one
and I wouldn't switch.
We're still having fun,
and you're still the one.

You're still the one
that makes me shout.
Still the one
that I dream about.
We're still having fun,
and you're still the one.

# Time After Time

## Cyndi Lauper

Lying

in my bed,

I hear

the clock

tick

and

think of you.

Caught up

in circles.

Confusion is

nothing

new.

Flashback.

Warm nights.

Almost left

behind.

Suitcases of

memories.

Time after—

Sometimes

you picture me;

I'm walking
too far ahead.
You're calling
to me.

Can't hear
what you've said.
Then you say,
"Go slow."
I fall
behind.

The
second hand
unwinds.

If you're lost,
you can look,
and you will find me.
Time after time.
If you fall,
I will catch you;
I'll be waiting.
Time after time.

After
my picture

fades

and darkness

has turned to

gray—

Watching

through windows,

you're

wondering

if I'm okay.

Secrets stolen from

deep

inside.

**64**

The drum

beats out

of time.


If you're lost,

you can look,

and you will find me.

Time after time.

If you fall,

I will catch you;

I'll be waiting.

Time after time.


Time after time—

# like a Virgin

Madonna

I made it through the wilderness.
Somehow, I made it through.
Didn't know how lost I was
until I found you.

I was beat—incomplete.
I'd been had.
I was sad and blue.
But you made me feel—
Yeah, you made me feel—
Shiny and new.

Like a virgin,
touched for the very first time.
Like a virgin,
when your heart beats next to mine.

Gonna give you all my love, boy.
My fear is fading fast.
Been saving it all for you,
'cause only love can last.

You're so fine and you're mine.
Make me strong—yeah you make me bold.
Oh, your love thawed out.
Yeah, your love thawed out
what was scared and cold.

Like a virgin,
touched for the very first time.
Like a virgin,
with your heartbeat next to mine.

You're so fine, and you're mine.
I'll be yours 'til the end of time.
'Cause you made me feel—
Yeah, you made me feel—
I've nothing to hide.

Like a virgin,
touched for the very first time.
Like a virgin,
with your heartbeat next to mine.

Like a virgin, ooh, ooh, like a virgin.
Feels so good inside.
When you hold me,
and your heart beats,

and you love me.

Oh, oh, oh, oh,
oh, oh, oh, oh, oh—
Ooh, baby.
Can't you hear my heart beat
for the very first time?

# Woman in love

Barbra Streisand

Life is a moment in space.
  When the dream is gone,
it's a lonelier place.

I kiss the morning good-bye.
  But down inside, you know
we never know why.

The road is narrow and long
  when eyes meet eyes
and the feeling is strong.

I turn away from the wall.
  I stumble and fall,
but I give you it all.

I am a woman in love
  and I'd do anything
to get you into my world

and hold you within.
  It's a right I defend
over and over again.

With you eternally mine,
   in love there is
no measure of time.

We planned it all at the start,
   that you and I
live in each other's hearts.

We may be oceans away.
   You feel my love.
I hear what you say.

The truth is ever a lie.
   I stumble and fall,
but I give you it all.

I am a woman in love
   and I'm talkin' to you.
I know how you feel

what a woman can do.
   It's a right I defend
over and over again.

# Sweet Emotion

## Aerosmith

Sweet emotion. Sweet emotion.
You talk about things that nobody cares.
You wearin' out things that nobody wears.
You're callin' my name but I gotta make clear,
I can't say, baby, where I'll be in a year.
Some sweet talkin' mama with a face like a gent,
said my get up and go must have got up and went.
Well, I got good news, she's a real good liar,
'cause my backstage boogie set yo' pants on fire.

Sweet emotion. Sweet emotion.
I pulled into town in a police car;
Your daddy said I took you just a little too far.
You're tellin' her things but your girlfriend lied.
You can't catch me 'cause the rabbit done died.
Standin' in the front just a shakin' your ass.
I'll take you backstage, you can drink from my glass.
I'm talking 'bout somethin' you can sure understand,
'Cause a month on the road
and I'll be eatin' from your hand.

Sweet emotion. Sweet emotion.

# Glory of love

Peter Cetera

Tonight it's very clear as we're both standing here.

There's so many things I want to say.

I will always love you, I will never leave you alone.

Sometimes I just forget, say things I might regret,

it breaks my heart to see you crying.

I don't want to lose you. I could never make it alone.

I am a man who would fight for your honor.

I'll be the hero you're dreaming of.

We'll live forever, knowing together,

that we did it all for the glory of love.

You keep me standing tall, you help me through it all,

I'm always strong when you're beside me.

I have always needed you, I could never make it alone.

Just like a knight in shining armor, from a long time ago,

just in time I will save the day, take you to my castle far away.

I am the man who will fight for your honor,

I'll be the hero that you're dreaming of.

We're gonna live forever, knowing together

that we did it all for the glory of love.

We'll live forever, knowing together,

that we did it all for the glory of love.

We did it all for love.

# Tonight I Celebrate My Love

Peabo Bryson and Roberta Flack

Tonight,
I celebrate
my love for you;
it seems the natural thing to do.

Tonight,
no one's gonna find us,
we'll have the world behind us,
when I make love to you.

Tonight,
I celebrate
my love for you;
and hope that deep inside
you'll feel it too.

Tonight,
our spirits
will be climbing
to a sky lit up with diamonds
when I make love to you
tonight.

Tonight,
I celebrate
my love for you,
and the midnight sun
is gonna come shining through.

Tonight,
there'll be
no distance between us.
What I want most to do
is to get close to you
tonight.

Tonight,
I celebrate
my love for you.
And soon this old world
will seem brand new.

Tonight,
we will both discover
how friends turn into lovers
when I make love to you
tonight.

# We Belong

Pat Benetar

Many times I've tried to tell you,
  many times I've cried alone.
Always I'm surprised how well
  you cut my feelings to the bone.

Don't wanna leave you really,
  I've invested too much time.
To give you up that easy
  to the doubts that complicate your mind.

We belong to the light,
  we belong to the thunder.
We belong to the sound
  of the words we've both fallen under.

Whatever we deny or embrace,
  for worse or for better,
we belong, we belong,
  we belong together.

Maybe it's a sign of weakness
  when I don't know what to say.

Maybe I just wouldn't know
    what to do with my strength, anyway.

Have we become a habit?
    Do we distort the facts?
Now there's no looking forward,
    now there's no turning back.

When you say close your eyes and try to sleep now,
    close your eyes and try to dream.
Clear your mind and do your best
    to try and wash the palette clean.

We can't begin to know it,
    how much we really care.
I hear your voice inside me,
    see your face everywhere. Still you say,

We belong to the light,
    we belong to the thunder.
We belong to the sound
    of the words we've both fallen under.

Whatever we deny or embrace,
    for worse or for better,
we belong, we belong,
    we belong together.

# Have You Ever Really Loved a Woman?

Bryan Adams

To really love a woman, to understand her,
 you gotta know her deep inside.
 Hear every thought.  See every dream.
 And give her wings when she wants to fly.
 Then, when you find yourself lying helpless in her arms,
 you know you really love a woman.

When you love a woman, you tell her that she's really wanted.
 When you love a woman, you tell her that she's the one.
 Cause she needs somebody to tell her that it's gonna last forever.

So tell me: Have you ever really, really, really ever loved a woman?

To really love a woman, let her hold you
 until you know how she needs to be touched.
 You've got to breathe her, really taste her,
 until you can feel her in your blood.
 And when you can see your unborn children in her eyes,
 you know you really love a woman.

When you love a woman, you tell her that she's really wanted.

When you love a woman, you tell her that she's the one.

Cause she needs somebody to tell her that you'll always be together.

So tell me: Have you ever really, really, really ever loved a woman?

You got to give her some faith. Hold her tight.

A little tenderness—got to treat her right.

She will be there for you, taking good care of you.

You really gotta love your woman.

# Islands in the Stream

## Kenny Rogers and Dolly Parton

Baby, when I met you,

there was peace unknown.

I set out to get you

with a fine tooth comb.

I was soft inside,

there was something goin' on.


You do something to me

that I can't explain.

Hold me closer

and I feel no pain.

Every beat of my heart,

We got something going on.


Tender love is blind.

It requires no dedication.

All this love we feel

needs no conversation.

We can ride it together (a-ha),

Making love with each other (a-ha).

Islands in the stream,

      that is what we are.

No one in between,

      how can we be wrong?

Sail away with me

      to another world,

and we rely on each other (a-ha).

      From one lover to another (a-ha).


I can live without you

      if the love was gone.

      Everything is nothing

if you got no one.

      And you just walk in the night,

      slowly losing sight of the real thing.

But that won't happen to us

      and we got no doubt,

      too deep in loving

we got no way out.

      And the message is clear:

      This could be the year for the real thing.


No more will you cry.

      Baby, I will hurt you never.

We start and end

as one in love, forever.

We can ride it together (a-ha).

Making love with each other (a-ha).


Islands in the stream,

that is what we are.

No one in between,

how can we be wrong?

Sail away with me

to another world,

and we rely on each other (a-ha).

From one lover to another (a-ha).

# Better Be Good to Me

Tina Turner

A prisoner
of your love,
entangled
in your web.

Hot whispers
in the night.
I'm captured
by your spell.
Captured.
Oh, yes,
I'm touched
by this show of
emotion.
Should I
be fractured
by your lack of
devotion?
Should I?

Should I?

You better

be good to me.

That's how

it's gotta

be now.

Cause I don't

have no use

for what

you loosely

call the truth.

Oh, you better

be good to me.


I think it's also right

that we don't need to fight.

We stand face to face

and you present your case.


And I know

you keep

telling me that

you love me.

And I really

do want to

believe,

but did you

think I'd
just accept you
in blind faith?

Oh, sure, babe,
anything
to please you.

You better
be good to me.
That's how
it's gotta
be now.
Cause I don't
have the time
for your
over-loaded lines.
You better
be good to me.

And I really don't see
why it's so hard to be
good to me.

And I don't understand.
What's your plan?

That you can't be
good to me?

What I can't feel,
I surely cannot see.

Why can't you be
good to me?
And if it's not real,
I do not wish to see.

Why can't you be
good to me?

# Afternoon Delight

## Starlight Vocal Band

Gonna find my baby,

    gonna hold her tight.

Gonna grab some afternoon delight.

    My motto's always been:

When it's right, it's right.

    Why wait until the middle of a cold dark night

when everything's a little clearer in the light of day?

    And we know the night is always gonna be there, anyway?


Thinking of you's working up my appetite.

    Looking forward to a little afternoon delight.

Rubbing sticks and stones together makes the sparks ignite.

    And the thought of loving you is getting so exciting.

Sky rockets in flight.

    Afternoon delight.

    Afternoon delight.

    Afternoon delight.


Started out this morning feeling so polite.

    I always though a fish could not be caught who wouldn't bite.

But you've got some bait a-waiting and I think I might

    try nibbling a little afternoon delight.

Sky rockets in flight.

    Afternoon delight.

    Afternoon delight.

    Afternoon delight.


Please be waiting for me, baby,

    when I come around.

We could make a lot of loving

    before the sun goes down.


Thinking of you's working up my appetite

    Looking forward to a little afternoon delight.

Rubbing sticks and stones together makes the sparks ignite.

    And the thought of loving you is getting so exciting.

Sky rockets in flight.

    Afternoon delight.

    Afternoon delight.

    Afternoon delight.

# Can't Get Enough of Your Love, Babe

## Barry White

I've heard people say that too much of anything is no good for you,
baby. But I don't know what I think. There's many times that we've
loved and we've shared love and made love. It doesn't seem to me
like it's enough. There's just not enough of it. There's just not
enough.

Oh, oh, babe.

My darling, I
    can't get enough of your love, babe.
Girl, I don't know, I don't know why I
    can't get enough of your love, babe.
Oh, some things I can't get used to—
    no matter how I try.
Just like the more you give, the more I want.
    And, baby, that's no lie.

Oh, no, babe. Tell me, what can I say?
    What am I gonna do?
How should I feel
    when everything is you?
What kind of love is this

that you're giving me?

Is it in your kiss

or just because you're sweet?


Girl, all I know is every time you're here, I feel the change.

Something moves. I scream your name. Do whatcha got to do.


Darling, I

can't get enough of your love, babe.

Girl, I don't know, I don't know, I don't know why I

can't get enough of your love, babe.

Oh, no, babe, girl, if only I could make you see

and make you understand, girl—

Your love for me is all I need.

And more than I can stand.


Oh, well, babe.


How can I explain

all the things I feel?

You've given me so much.

Girl, you're so unreal.

Still I keep loving you,

more and more each time.

Girl, what am I gonna do?

Because you blow my mind.

I get the same old feeling every time you're here. I feel the change.

Something moves, I scream your name. Do whatcha got to do.

Darling, I

can't get enough of your love, babe.

Oh, no, babe.

Baby, let me take all of my life to find you.

But you can believe it's gonna take the rest of my life to keep you.

Oh, no, babe.

My darling, I

can't get enough of your love, babe.

Yeah, I don't know, I don't know, I don't know why

can't get enough of your love, babe.

Oh, my darling, I can't get enough of your love, babe.

Girl, I can't get enough of your love, babe—

# Index of first lines

A prisoner of your love 81

Baby, when I met you 78

Dance with me, I want to be your partner 38

Every time I think of you 52

Gonna find my baby, gonna hold her tight 85

I can't fight this feeling any longer 36
I can't stop this feeling deep inside of me 42
I know just how to whisper 20
I made it through the wilderness 65
I wake up every morning 25
I'm lying alone 56
I'm saying all the things that I know you'll like 50
I'm sleeping 18
I've heard people say that too much of anything
is no good for you, baby 87
I've been lonely 40
I've never seen you looking so lovely as you did tonight 23

Life is a moment in space 68
Lying in my bed 62

Many times I've tried to tell you                                          74

Maybe I hang around here                                                   10


Saying "I love you" is not the words I want to hear from you               39

Shadows falling, baby, we stand alone                                      30

She's got a smile that it seems to me                                      54

Sitting here, eating my heart out, waiting—                                28

Sweet emotion. Sweet emotion                                               70


There's a port                                                             12

To really love a woman, to understand her                                  76

Tonight I celebrate my love for you                                        72

Tonight it's very clear as we're both standing here                        71


Watching every motion in my foolish lover's game                           44

Well, I'm hot blooded                                                      33

We've been together since way back when                                    59


You ask me if I love you                                                   46

You know our love was meant to be                                          48

Your love is like bad medicine                                             15

# About the Authors

**Afternoon Delight**
Words and Music by Bill Danoff
Copyright © 1976 Cherry Lane Music
Publishing Company, Inc. (ASCAP) and
DreamWorks Songs (ASCAP)
Worldwide Rights for DreamWorks Songs
Administered by Cherry Lane Music
Publishing Company, Inc.
International Copyright Secured
All Rights Reserved

**All Out of Love**
Words and Music by Graham Russell and
Clive Davis
Copyright © 1980 by Nottsongs
All Rights Administered by Careers-BMG
Music Publishing, Inc.
International Copyright Secured
All Rights Reserved

**Bad Medicine**
Words and Music by Desmond Child,
Richie Sambora and Jon Bon Jovi
© 1988 EMI APRIL MUSIC INC.,
DESMOBILE MUSIC CO., INC., UNIVERSAL -
POLYGRAM INTERNATIONAL PUBLISHING,
INC., BON JOVI PUBLISHING and NEW JER-
SEY UNDERGROUND MUSIC INC.
All Rights for DESMOBILE MUSIC CO., INC.
Controlled and Administered by EMI APRIL
MUSIC INC.
International Copyright Secured
Used by Permission
All Rights Reserved

**Better Be Good to Me**
Words and Music by Mike Chapman,
Nicky Chinn and Holly Knight
Copyright © 1981 by BMG Songs, Inc.
International Copyright Secured
All Rights Reserved

**Brandy (You're a Fine Girl)**
Words and Music by Elliot Lurie
Copyright © 1971 by Evie Music, Inc. and
Spruce Run Music
Copyright Renewed
All Rights Administered by Chappell & Co.
International Copyright Secured
All Rights Reserved

**Can't Fight This Feeling**
Words and Music by Kevin Cronin
Copyright © 1984 Fate Music (ASCAP)
International Copyright Secured
All Rights Reserved

**Can't Get Enough of Your Love, Babe**
Words and Music by Barry White
Copyright © 1974 by
Unichappell Music Inc.
International Copyright Secured
All Rights Reserved

**Dance with Me**
Words and Music by John and
Johanna Hall
© 1975 EMI BLACKWOOD MUSIC INC.
and SIREN SONGS

### Glory of Love

Theme from Karate Kid Part II
Words and Music by David Foster, Peter
Cetera and Diane Nini
Copyright © 1986 by Air Bear Music, BMG
Songs, Inc., EMI Gold Horizon Music Corp.
and EMI Golden Torch Music Corp.
All Rights for Air Bear Music Administered
by Peermusic Ltd.
International Copyright Secured
All Rights Reserved

### Guilty

Words and Music by Barry Gibb, Maurice
Gibb and Robin Gibb
Copyright © 1980 by Gibb Brothers Music
All Rights Administered by Careers-BMG
Music Publishing, Inc.
International Copyright Secured
All Rights Reserved

### Have You Ever Really Loved a Woman?

from the Motion Picture Don Juan DeMarco
Words and Music by Bryan Adams,
Michael Kamen and Robert John Lange
Copyright © 1994 Badams Music Ltd.,
Sony/ATV Songs LLC, New Line Music, K-
Man Corp. and Zomba Enterprises, Inc.
All Rights on behalf of Badams Music Ltd.,
Sony/ATV Songs LLC, New Line Music and
K-Man Corp. Administered by Sony/ATV

Music Publishing, 8 Music Square West,
Nashville, TN 37203
International Copyright Secured
All Rights Reserved

### Hooked on a Feeling

Words and Music by Mark James
© 1968 (Renewed 1996) SCREEN GEMS-
EMI MUSIC INC.
International Copyright Secured
Used by Permission
All Rights Reserved

### Hot Blooded

Words and Music by Mick Jones and
Lou Gramm
Copyright © 1980 Somerset Songs
Publishing, Inc.
International Copyright Secured
All Rights Reserved

### Hot Stuff

Words and Music by Pete Bellotte, Harold
Faltermeyer and Keith Forsey
Copyright © 1979 by Intersong U.S.A., Inc.
and Budde Music, Inc.
All Rights Administered by Intersong
U.S.A., Inc.
International Copyright Secured
All Rights Reserved

### I Honestly Love You

Words and Music by Peter Allen
and Jeff Barry
Copyright © 1974 IRVING MUSIC, INC.,
WOOLNOUGH MUSIC and JEFF BARRY
INTERNATIONAL

All Rights Administered by
IRVING MUSIC, INC.

**I Think I Love You**
featured in the Television Series The
Partridge Family
Words and Music by Tony Romeo
© 1970 (Renewed 1998) SCREEN GEMS-
EMI MUSIC INC.

**Islands in the Stream**
Words and Music by Barry Gibb, Maurice
Gibb and Robin Gibb
Copyright © 1983 by Gibb Brothers Music
All Rights for the U.S. Administered by
Careers-BMG Music Publishing, Inc.

94

**Lady in Red**
Words and Music by Chris de Burgh
Copyright © 1986 RONDOR MUSIC (LON-
DON) LTD.
All Rights in the USA and Canada
Administered by RUMO MUSIC CORP.

**Like a Virgin**
Words and Music by Billy Steinberg and
Tom Kelly
Copyright © 1984 Sony/ATV Tunes LLC
All Rights Administered by Sony/ATV Music
Publishing, 8 Music Square West,
Nashville, TN 37203

**Making Love Out of Nothing at All**
Words and Music by Jim Steinman
Copyright © 1983 by Lost Boys Music
All Rights for the U.S. and Canada
Administered by Edward B. Marks
Music Company

**Missing You**
Words and Music by John Waite, Charles
Sanford and Mark Leonard
Copyright © 1984 by Paperwaite Music,
Fallwater Music and Markmeem Music
All Rights for Paperwaite Music
Administered by Alley Music Corp. and
Trio Music Company, Inc.
All Rights for Fallwater Music Administered
by WB Music Corp.

**More Than Words**
Words and Music by Nuno Bettencourt
and Gary Cherone
Copyright © 1990 COLOR ME BLIND MUSIC
All Rights Administered by
RUMO MUSIC CORP.

**Morning Train (Nine to Five)**
Words and Music by Florrie Palmer
Copyright © 1981 by Pendulum Music Ltd.

**Physical**
Words and Music by Stephen A. Kipner
and Terry Shaddick

**Sometimes When We Touch**
Words by Dan Hill
Music by Barry Mann

**Still the One**
Words and Music by John Hall and
Johanna Hall

**Sweet Child O' Mine**
Words and Music by W. Axl Rose,
Slash, Izzy Stradlin', Duff McKagan and
Steven Adler

**Sweet Emotion**
Words and Music by Steven Tyler and
Tom Hamilton

**Take My Breath Away (Love Theme)**
from the Paramount Picture Top Gun
Words and Music by Giorgio Moroder and
Tom Whitlock

**Time After Time**
Words and Music by Cyndi Lauper and
Rob Hyman